LIL' ANGEL TOMMY

Lil' Angel Tommy

By Lawrence Weeks

Illustrations by: Kyla Newman

© 2017

INTRODUCTION

Imagine you were in a foreign, noisy, and crowed city at night, not understanding the language spoken, recognizing only a few words, but not really comprehending any situations taking place around you, wanting to express a need for help, but not being able to. This experience may begin to help you relate to what a child with autism feels on an ordinary day.

LIL' ANGEL TOMMY

Sure, there are Angels in Heaven, different kinds too . . . big ones, small ones, smart ones, gifted ones, and some very special ones who are very dear to God, ones over whom God keeps a special watch.

Our story is about a special autistic Angel named Lil' Angel Tommy who had a most wonderful smile and who loved to play with heavenly sticks of all sizes.

Lil' Angel Tommy had three sisters, who watched over him and helped him with all his Angelic chores. His sisters, Angel Kyla, Angel Emily, and Angel Lindey would help him clean up their cloud that they called home, a beautiful cloud all puffy and fluffy, high up in the sunny blue sky.

One day, the word came down that God was going to have a very special day in December that needed every Angel's attention. God didn't say exactly what was going to happen, but He said it was very special. And He wanted all the Angels to be ready for this big event.

So, all the Angels got together to get their best gowns and halos ready for whatever it was that was going to happen. Lil' Angel Tommy's sisters were all busy cleaning everything, and he helped as much as he could.

"We gotta' get our gowns all cleaned and ironed, "said Angel Kyla.

"And don't forget our halos, too," reminded Angel Emily.

So, off they went scrubbing, cleaning, and ironing everything they could find to get ready for God's big surprise. And they all wondered what it could be.

The Angelic choir decided to get together to try out their voices. So, Lil' Angel Tommy and his sisters went to the choir practice.

5

Their voices sounded magnificent. Lil' Angel Tommy did his best to sing, but since he couldn't sing like his sisters, he ran in circles, and flapped his hands while holding a long stick the size of a long rod, and jumped up and down to the music.

THE GOWNS

Lil' Angel Tommy's sisters put his newly cleaned gown on him, and he proudly danced about holding his stick, showing everybody how pretty and clean his gown was. Each of them put their initials on their gowns so they wouldn't get them confused.

Sister Angel Kyla had a "A K," Angel Emily had an "A E," and Angel Lindey had an "A L", each on the bottoms of their gowns.

Lil' Angel Tommy had a bright "L A T" sewn on the bottom of his gown. He was so proud of that.

WHERE WAS THIS EVENT TO BE?

All the Angels in Heaven were very excited and wondered about whatever God had planned, so they were all busy getting ready.

Everybody's halos were sparkling, and everyone was all ready for the big event.

God told all His Angels to go to a small village to the south of Jerusalem in a little town called Bethlehem.

They were told to follow a star, the Star of Bethlehem mentioned in the Bible:

> Oh Beautiful Star (Beautiful, Beautiful Star)
> Of Bethlehem (Star of Bethlehem)
> Shine upon us until the glory dawns
> Give us the light to light the way
> Unto the land of perfect day
> Beautiful Star of Bethlehem, shine on
>
> Beautiful Star the hope of light
> Guiding the pilgrims through the night
> Over the mountains 'til the break of dawn
> Into the light of perfect day
> It will give out a lovely ray
> Beautiful Star of Bethlehem, shine on

And God wanted the Angels to also practice singing this song:

We Three Kings

♪ O star of wonder, star of night,
Star with royal beauty bright,
Westward leading, still proceeding,
Guide us to thy perfect light
Westward leading, still proceeding,
Guide us to thy perfect light. ♪

So, Lil' Angel Tommy's sisters practiced every day with Tommy softly dancing around and clapping his hands. The little Angels all sounded great and had lots of fun. What was the big deal in December they all wondered?

Much had been done. And now they and all the rest of the Angels were ready to head off to Bethlehem for the big event.

THE FLIGHT TO BETHLEHEM

Dozens, if not hundreds, if not thousands, if not millions of Angels gathered from all the clouds of Heaven and from all the stars in the universe for their journey to Bethlehem.

It was awesome to see all these Angels swooping and soaring through the Heavens, zooming past the stars, coming down from the clouds for the big event early on the morning of December 25.

Lil' Angel Tommy and his sisters soared and frolicked up and over and around the stars on their merry trip to Earth.

"Don't fly so close to the stars, Lil' Angel Tommy!" cautioned Angel Kyla.

"You might snag your gown on one of the star's points!"

Lil' Angel Tommy smiled at Angel Kyla and zoomed over, up, around, and past the stars as he flew by each of his sister Angels.

"Getting kinda' close to the pointed stars, Lil' Angel Tommy!" yelled Angel Emily. "Watch out!"

Lil' Angel Tommy flew a little too close to one of the stars, and his gown got snagged on one of its points. "Ripppp!" was heard by his sister Angels, and Lil' Angel Tommy's stick flew out of his hands!

They all paused next to the star to see that a big piece of Lil' Angel Tommy's gown was torn off the bottom. He also lost his long rod and started to cry.

He had hoped that his sisters' hard work to get them all ready wouldn't be ruined. But now his gown was torn and his stick was gone.

"There's not much we can do, Lil' Angel Tommy," said Angel Kyla. "We have to get to Bethlehem quickly. So, let's move on, ok?"

Lil' Angel Tommy looked sad and had his eyes down. He felt bad that the bottom of his gown was ruined. He wiped away some tears, and then held Angel Kyla's hand as they soared off to Bethlehem.

Dozens, if not hundreds, if not thousands, if not millions of Angels gathered from all the clouds of Heaven. It seemed that all the Seraphim, all the Cherubim, all the Archangels, and the Rules and Powers Angels filled the Heavens on their way toward Bethlehem.

It was grand and beautiful sight watching them head toward a small stable near an inn in the crowded city. And now it was even more crowded with all the wonderful angels. There were angels shepherds, sheep, and oxen all gathered around a manger.

BETHLEHEM

A man named Joseph went to a city called Bethlehem with his wife Mary. And when they got there, she brought forth her firstborn Son, and wrapped Him in swaddling clothes, and laid Him in a manger.

The three sister Angels and Lil' Angel Tommy found their way up to the front of the crowd. What God had planned for them to see was the birth of His Son, the birth of Jesus, the Savior of the World.

This is what all the Angels in Heaven were to get ready for along with shepherds of the field. Everyone was in awe at this moment.

Lil' Angel Tommy stood there with his sister Angels and was very sad because he was wearing a torn gown, and his favorite Heavenly rod had been lost way up in the clouds. But he looked with tears in his eyes at the beautiful sight in front of him:

The Virgin Mary was kneeling over the small manger where the Baby Jesus lay.

Angel Kyla looked at Joseph, Jesus' father standing behind the Mother and Child, and noticed something rather odd: the staff that Joseph held had a heavenly glow to it. She thought to herself, "That looks like the long stick that Lil' Angel Tommy had lost way up the Heavens."

It WAS Lil' Angel Tommy's Heavenly rod!

When Angel Kyla pointed it out to Lil' Angel Tommy, he started to get a big smile on his face, but still had some tears from his having a torn gown for this very special occasion.

Mother Mary looked up at Lil' Angel Tommy and motioned for him to come forward to get a closer look at Baby Jesus. Lil' Angel Tommy wasn't sure what to do. Mother Mary smiled again and urged Lil' Angel Tommy to come forward.

So, Lil' Angel Tommy stepped forward to the Baby Jesus to get a good look. There was the Baby Jesus before him all bundled in swaddling wrap.

Something caught Lil' Angel Tommy's eyes. In the corner of Baby Jesus' swaddling clothes was something that kind of sparkled . . . the letters "LAT" were clearly visible. Somehow Mother Mary had found Lil' Angel Tommy's piece of torn gown and used it to wrap Lil' Baby Jesus for this incredible moment.

Lil' Angel Tommy's eyes sparkled and a big grin came over his face. His sisters' eyes also filled with tears of happiness too. What a wonderful surprise for Baby Jesus' birthday. The piece of Lil' Angel Tommy's torn gown was now wrapping the Baby Jesus!

What a wonderful Christmas present for the Baby Jesus!

Just then dozens, if not hundreds, if not thousands, if not millions of Angels burst into song:

♪ O Holy night, the stars are brightly shining
It is the night of our dear Savior's birth
Long lay the world in sin and error pining
'Til He appeared and the soul felt it's worth
A thrill of hope the weary world rejoices
For yonder breaks a new and glorious morn
Fall on your knees

O hear the angel voices
O night divine
O night when Christ was born
O night divine
O night, o night divine
O night, O Holy Night, O night divine!
O night, O Holy Night, O night divine! ♪

The three sister Angels sang and sang along with the other Angels, and Lil' Tommy Angel danced around and tears came to his eyes. He looked at the baby in the manger, smiled, and softly said, "Jesus."

And a Merry Christ-filled Christmas to all, and Lil' Tommy Angel played a wonderful part in Jesus' story!

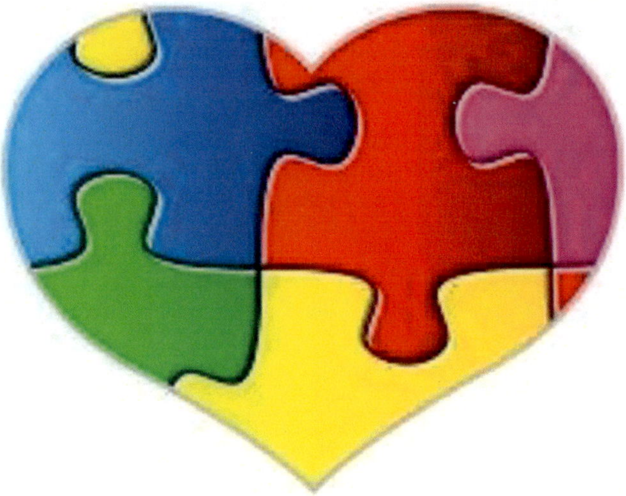

Momma Jenny and Lil' Tommy

A LITTLE ABOUT TOMMY

Tommy is diagnosed with nonverbal autism. He has about 5-10 "words/sounds". He is learning to communicate with icon cards (PECS) and AAC apps on the iPad. He gets speech therapy and occupational therapy at school and privately once a week. Although Tommy wants to talk, he physically and mentally cannot... YET. Occupational therapy helps with day-to-day living activities and fine motor skills. With the help of his teachers, therapists, and with home support, he does the best he can and never gives up!

Tommy is an energetic, smart, silly, fun loving, 6-year-old. He is the youngest of four children. Tommy loves sticks, he loves to build teepees, and carry sticks around. He loves the water, everything from swimming to river walking! He loves cuddling with his dad and watching him play video games! Tommy loves to build with his train tracks, watch trains and firetrucks on YouTube! Tommy's favorite movie is Happy Feet! Tommy loves playing with his sisters, going to camp, and to school! His preschool teachers (Miss. G, Miss. R, and Miss V) were amazing last year; they always went above and beyond to help him and never gave up on him!

Kyla my illustrator and me

    This little Christmas Story is one that I have had in my mind since I was in grade school, many years ago. With the help of Tommy's sister Kyla and Tommy's mother, Jenna, I've put the story to pen and paper and am proud of the result. I hope you like it.

Made in the USA
Lexington, KY
15 November 2017